MICHELANGELO

Lives
of the Artists

MICHELANGELO

Gareth Stevens Publishing
A WORLD ALMANAC EDUCATION GROUP COMPANY

Please visit our web site at:
www.worldalmanaclibrary.com
For a free color catalog describing World Almanac®
Library's list of high-quality books and multimedia
programs, call 1-800-848-2928 (USA) or 1-800-387-3178
(Canada). World Almanac® Library's fax: (414) 332-3567.

Library of Congress Cataloging-in-Publication Data available upon request
from publisher. Fax (414) 336-0157 for the attention of the Publishing
Records Department.

ISBN 0-8368-5600-7 (lib. bdg.)
ISBN 0-8368-5605-8 (softcover)

This North American edition first published in 2004 by
World Almanac® Library
330 West Olive Street, Suite 100
Milwaukee, WI 53212 USA

The series "The Lives of the Artists"
was created and produced by McRae Books Srl
Borgo Santa Croce, 8 – Florence (Italy)
info@mcraebooks.com
Publishers: Anne McRae and Marco Nardi

Project Editor: Loredana Agosta
Art History consultant: Roberto Carvalho de Magalhães
Text: Sean Connolly
Illustrations: Studio Stalio (Alessandro Cantucci,
Fabiano Fabbrucci, Andrea Morandi)
Graphic Design: Marco Nardi
Picture Research: Loredana Agosta
Layout: Studio Yotto
World Almanac® Library editor: JoAnn Early Macken
World Almanac® Library art direction: Tammy Gruenewald

Acknowledgments
All efforts have been made to obtain and provide compensation for the
copyright to the photographs and artworks in this book in accordance
with legal provisions. Persons who may nevertheless still have claims are
requested to contact the copyright owners.

t=top; tl=top left; tc=top center; tr=top right; c=center; cl=center left; cr=
center right; b=bottom; bl=bottom left; bc=bottom center; br=bottom right

The publishers would like to thank the following museums and archives
who have authorized the reproduction of the works in this book:
The Bridgeman Art Library, London / Farabola Foto, Milano: 13t, 13b, 15b,
17br, 17cr, 23t, 25t, 26cr, 27br, 40cl, 43t, 43c, 45cl; Foto Scala, Florence: cover,
3, 7tr, 9tr, 9cr, 9bl, 11t, 11br, 12cr, 13t, 15tr, 17l, 18r, 19cl, 22, 28c, 29t, 30bl, 31t,
31cr, 33tr, 37b, 42cr, 44; Foto Musei Vaticani: 5, 20–21, 21t, 24b, 32, 34–35, 35;
Archivio Electa, Milano: 39b, 41t, 41c; Erich Lessing / Contrasto, Milano: 45b

Printed in Hong Kong

1 2 3 4 5 6 7 8 9 08 07 06 05 04

cover: *The Holy Family* (detail), Uffizi, Florence

opposite: *The Last Judgment* (detail), The Sistine Chapel, Vatican

previous page: *The Holy Family*, Uffizi, Florence

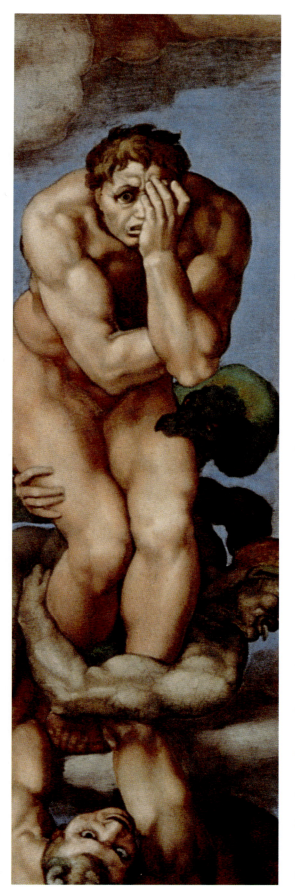

Table of Contents

Introduction   6

Young Michelangelo   8

Roots of Stone   10

New Life   12

A Tender Masterpiece   14

A Proud Symbol   16

Missed Opportunities   18

The Sistine Ceiling   20

Adjoining Geniuses   24

Return to Stone   26

Summoned Back to Florence   28

Breakthroughs in Architecture   30

The Last Judgment   32

Spiritual Struggles   36

An Architect of Rome   38

A Crowning Achievement   40

Sorrowful Old Age   42

The Legacy of Michelangelo   44

Glossary and Index   46-48

Introduction

Michelangelo's Life (An Overview)
1475 Michelangelo Buonarotti is born in Caprese, near Florence.
1487 He enters Ghirlandaio's workshop as an apprentice to learn fresco painting.
1489–92 He is taken up by Lorenzo de' Medici, the most powerful man in Florence, a humanist and patron of the arts. Lives at his house until Lorenzo dies in 1492.
1494 Works in Bologna.
1496–1501 In Rome, where he sculpts the *Pietà*.
1504 Completes the statue of *David* in Florence.
1505 In Rome, at work on the tomb of Pope Julius II.
1508 Begins the frescoes on the ceiling of the Sistine Chapel in Rome.
1516–20 Working on Pope Julius II's tomb (Rome) and the façade of San Lorenzo in Florence.
c. 1520 Works on the New Sacristy in of San Lorenzo.
1527–30 The Medici leave Florence. The artist supports the Republic against the Medici.
1530 Return of the Medici. Continues work on their tomb in the New Sacristy.
1532 In Rome, working on Pope Julius II's tomb.
1536–41 Paints *The Last Judgment* fresco in the Sistine Chapel.
1536–47 Friendship with Vittoria Colonna.
1546 Begins building St. Peter's Basilica in Rome.
1564 Dies in Rome.

Michelangelo di Lodovico Buonarroti Simoni is remembered as one of the greatest artists of all time. He became famous during his lifetime for the striking and original art he created, for which he was alternately admired and ridiculed by his contemporaries. Michelangelo was a versatile artistic genius who worked as a sculptor, painter, architect, and poet. Born into a family of noble lineage, he moved easily in powerful circles. But even when he became rich, he maintained a modest lifestyle and stayed totally dedicated to his art. He lived during the Renaissance, an important age of change and discovery. His own contribution was to change the way both art and the artist were seen.

▲ The Birth of Venus (c. 1485) by Sandro Botticelli (1446–1510) epitomized the works commissioned by the Medici and other Florentine families during Michelangelo's childhood.

▲ *Bronze portrait of Michelangelo by Daniele da Volterra (c. 1509–1566).*

Michelangelo the Sculptor

Michelangelo thought of himself first as a sculptor rather than a painter. When Pope Julius II (1443–1513) asked him to paint the ceiling of the Sistine Chapel, the artist told him that he was not a good enough painter for the job! Michelangelo sculpted throughout his lifetime, working in wood, bronze, and marble. His most famous sculptures include the *Pietà*, *David*, and the *Medici Madonna*, shown here. When Michelangelo died at the age of eighty-nine, he was hard at work on a statue.

◄ *Michelangelo worked on the* Medici Madonna *in Florence from 1521 to 1531 after spending fourteen triumphant years in Rome. The Madonna was part of the tombs he designed for the Medici.*

Michelangelo's ITALY
Venice
Bologna
Florence
Rome

Michelangelo the Man

Michelangelo was a passionate and emotional man, capable of great warmth and kindness. He was also stubborn, difficult, and even cruel when he lost his temper. He never married, but he had intense friendships with both men and women during his long life.

▶ The Holy Family with St. John the Baptist *(c. 1504), is usually known as the* Doni Tondo *after Agnolo Doni, who commissioned the work.*

Michelangelo the Painter

The artist is most well known as a painter for his works in the Sistine Chapel in Rome. He painted the *Sistine Ceiling*, showing scenes and personages from the *Old Testament*, in 1508–12 for Pope Julius II. Returning in 1534, he painted the *Last Judgment* on the west wall of the chapel. These frescoes are considered to be among the greatest works in the history of Western painting. They were restored in the 1980s and 1990s.

Florence

▶ *The florin, which took its name from Florence, was one of the strongest currencies in Renaissance Europe.*

During Michelangelo's life, Florence was one of the richest and most powerful cities in Europe. Florentine merchants traded cloth and other products far and wide, developing an international banking system and laying the basis for modern accountancy and commerce. They spent their wealth on building magnificent churches and palazzi (large city houses) and commissioning works of art. The Renaissance began in Florence.

▼ *A view of Florence in the 1480s, based on a woodcut by Francesco di Lorenzo Rosselli (1448–1513). It shows some of the places where Michelangelo lived or worked during the early part of his life.*

Michelangelo's Florence

Settignano

Santa Maria Novella

Palazzo Medici-Riccardi, Via Larga

FIORENZA

Via Ghibellina

Via dei Bentaccordi

Young Michelangelo

1475 Michelangelo, second of five sons, is born to Lodovico Buonarroti.

c. 1488 In Florence, he enters a contract to work as an apprentice in Ghirlandaio's workshop. He proves to be a quick learner and works on the frescoes at the main altar of Santa Maria Novella with Ghirlandaio and the other painters of the workshop. He stays at the workshop for about a year.

Ghirlandaio

Domenico Ghirlandaio (1449–94) was a well-known painter in his mid-thirties when Michelangelo entered the workshop he ran with his brothers Davide and Benedetto. Ghirlandaio had worked in Rome with Botticelli as well as Pietro Perugino (c. 1450–1523) and Luca Signorelli (c. 1445–1523) before returning to Florence.

Michelangelo decided to become an artist when he was about ten. After a battle of wills with his father, who did not approve of his choice and who considered artists to be socially inferior, Michelangelo got his way. In Florence, he was apprenticed to the well-established artist Domenico Ghirlandaio to learn fresco painting. Michelangelo proved to be a willing and talented learner. Before long, he was excused from performing the more mundane chores normally assigned to apprentices and began contributing to the finished works of art produced by Ghirlandaio's successful workshop.

▶ *Between their chores, young apprentices learned the basics of drawing and painting in the artist's workshop.*

The Artist's Workshop

At the time of Michelangelo's childhood, great artists in Florence and other Italian cities operated from bottegas, or workshops, that have sometimes been described as "painting factories." Having established a reputation, an artist would receive far more commissions than he could execute alone. Apprentices, boys and young men learning the profession, would be assigned various chores such as mixing colors and preparing other materials. Talented apprentices would also paint sections of large panels or frescoes.

▲ *The Medici Palace (now Palazzo Medici-Riccardi) in Florence, built by Michelozzo (1396–1472). The young Michelangelo lived here with the Medici family from about 1489.*

FLORENCE: Town and Country

Many families moved from the countryside into Florence during the fourteenth and fifteenth centuries to take part in the explosion of industry and trade. They did not sell their ancestral lands, however, and a strong link between the city and its surrounding countryside was maintained. Michelangelo himself spent the first two years of his life with his wet nurse at Settignano, a village in the hills above Florence. His nurse was the wife and mother of stonemasons, and in later life, Michelangelo liked to say that he received his love of marble and stone as a nursling.

▲ *The Medici Villa at Cafaggiolo, built by Michelozzo beginning in 1444. The Medici family owned many splendid villas in the countryside near Florence and spent the hot summers out of town.*

Santa Maria Novella

The cycle of frescoes in the church of Santa Maria Novella, illustrating scenes from the lives of the Virgin and St. John the Baptist, was Ghirlandaio's most important work.
It was commissioned in 1485 by Giovanni Tornabuoni (1428–97), a partner in the powerful Florentine Medici bank.

▶ *This scene from the frescoes in the choir of Santa Maria Novella shows Herod's Feast. The scene is set in grandiose architecture of an elegant fifteenth-century court with a landscape in the background.*

▲ *Detail from Masaccio's frescoes in the Brancacci Chapel (c. 1427). He introduced a lightness of touch and naturalism.*

▼ *Michelangelo's drawing of two figures (c. 1490) is based on Giotto's* Ascension of St. John the Evangelist.

▶ *A detail of Giotto's fresco of the* Ascension of St. John the Evangelist *(1320), painted in Santa Croce, Florence.*

The Impact of Giotto and Masaccio

During his youth, Michelangelo was particularly inspired by earlier artists from his native city of Florence. He spent a great deal of time studying and copying the works of Giotto (1267–1337) and Masaccio (1401–28). He preferred the rooted simplicity of their works to the lighter style of Botticelli (see page 9) and other fashionable artists. Their influence is obvious in the statues Michelangelo executed in Bologna in 1494–5. Four years later, when he sculpted the *Pietà* (see page 15) in Rome, he had already acquired his own style.

Roots of Stone

1488–9 Michelangelo begins to tire of life in the Ghirlandaio workshop, having had the chance to contribute to several finished pieces.

c. 1489 Introduced by his friend and fellow Ghirlandaio apprentice Francesco Granacci (1469–1543), Michelangelo secures a place to learn sculpture in the art school in the gardens of the Medici family and leaves Ghirlandaio's workshop.

1489 He begins an intensive study of sculpture under the guidance of Bertoldo di Giovanni, an artist employed by the Medici and a former pupil of Donatello.

1489–92 Becomes a favorite of Lorenzo de' Medici. Sculpts the *Madonna of the Stairs*.

Michelangelo was talented and ambitious, and the work in the Ghirlandaio workshop soon became tiresome for him. Moreover, he wanted to try his hand at sculpture. He served only one of his three years as an apprentice and then found a place in the art school in the Medici gardens. At this time, he was taken up by Lorenzo de' Medici, the great patron of the arts, who was later given the title "Magnificent" because of his contributions to the cultural life of Florence. Living in the Medici household, Michelangelo learned about sculpture from Bertoldo di Giovanni (c. 1420–91), who himself had studied under the great Donatello (1386–1466).

▲ Donatello's David (c. 1430–46), the first nude statue of the Renaissance. The nearly life-sized bronze sculpture gave the biblical hero a sense of individuality as opposed to the stylized representations in sculpture before Donatello's time.

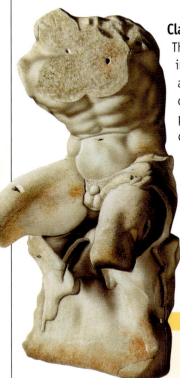

▲ Even this fragment of a classical sculpture bursts with energy and realism.

Classical Sculpture

The term *Renaissance* means "rebirth" in French — a good reflection of the attitude that Europeans had about their own past. Artists and enlightened patrons such as the Medici studied or collected classical works of art, especially sculptures. They could observe firsthand how sculptors from ancient Greece and Rome had worked stone into rounded and realistic depictions of the human form and character. Michelangelo was certainly inspired by the classical statues that the Medici had on display.

Donatello

Donatello was the greatest European sculptor of the fifteenth century and one of the artists who developed the Renaissance tradition in Florence. Inspired by the concrete, rounded figures by Giotto and by the sculpture of ancient Greece and Rome, Donatello gave new life to the human figure in sculpture, making it more realistic and less stylized than the sculptors before him.

Humanism

One of the most powerful ideas driving the Renaissance was that of humanism, the devotion to man's individuality and capacity to shape events. Before the Renaissance, Europeans believed that classical writing was only worth studying as a way of presenting the Christian message. Humanists, on the other hand, believed that these writings had value of their own. This view was developed in Florence by Marsilio Ficino (1433–99), who made the first complete translation of the works of the ancient Greek philosopher Plato (c. 428–c. 348 B.C.) into Latin. Supported by the Florentine statesman Cosimo de' Medici (1389–1464), Ficino established the Platonic Academy. Members of the Academy used Plato's writings to develop notions of Neoplatonism, which stressed the unity, goodness, and holiness of the universe.

▲ In his writings, Marsilio Ficino developed the idea that beyond the material universe is a greater reality.

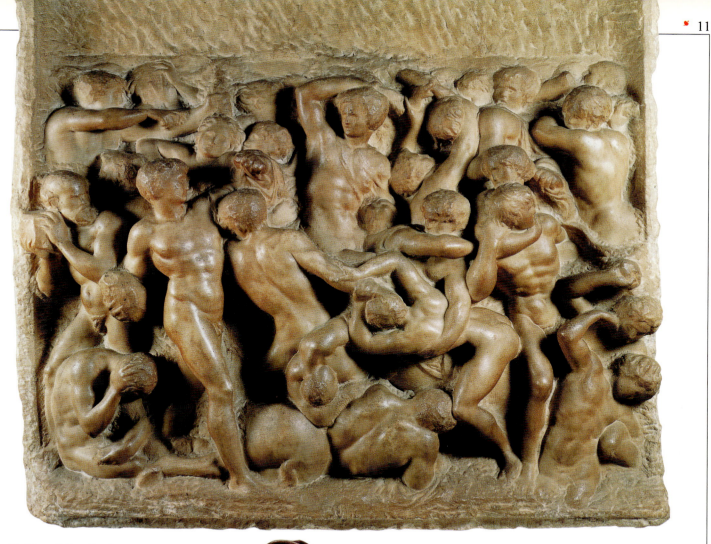

The Battle of the Centaurs

One of Michelangelo's very first works was the relief sculpture of *The Battle of the Centaurs* (c. 1492), above. It shows humans and centaurs (creatures with the head and chest of a man and the body of a horse) as they fight. The subject, a favorite with Greek and Roman artists, is about a wedding feast at which the centaurs misbehaved and were expelled. Michelangelo kept this work all his life.

▶ *Painted terracotta (baked earth) bust of* Lorenzo de' Medici *(c. 1480) by Andrea del Verrocchio.*

Lorenzo the Magnificent

Lorenzo de' Medici (1449–92) was the most brilliant member of the powerful banking family that ruled Florence for much of the fifteenth and sixteenth centuries. An important statesman, he also wrote poetry, collected works of Greek and Roman art, and encouraged artists and scholars. He helped many famous artists, including Botticelli, Andrea del Verrocchio (c. 1435–88), and Leonardo da Vinci (1452–1519).

▶ *This painting by Ottavio Vannini (1584–1644) shows Michelangelo (right) presenting a marble bust to Lorenzo the Magnificent (center).*

In Lorenzo's Garden

According to legend, Lorenzo was so impressed by Michelangelo's work in the Medici gardens that he invited the boy to live with his family. During this same period, Michelangelo got his distinctively-shaped nose by being too cheeky with a fellow student who punched him and broke it.

New Life

1492 Lorenzo de' Medici dies.
1494 Michelangelo, anxious about the French advance on Florence, leaves for Venice, then moves to Bologna.
1494 Revolts within Florence's Tuscan territories undermine the power of Lorenzo's successor Piero de' Medici. The sixty-year reign of the Medici is ended temporarily even before French King Charles VIII enters Florence.

After Lorenzo de' Medici's death, Michelangelo found himself without a patron. Lorenzo's son and successor Piero had little work for the young artist, so Michelangelo threw himself into a study of the human form to improve his technique in sculpture. He gained permission to study human corpses at the monastery hospital of Santo Spirito. His desire to celebrate the human form was at odds with the prevailing religious fervor sweeping Florence in the wake of Savonarola's increasing influence. The likely invasion by the French was a more direct threat to Michelangelo's artistic well-being, and in 1494 he left Florence for Venice and then Bologna.

▶ *This pen-and-pencil drawing of a nude figure dates from about 1504. It shows how Michelangelo's studies of the human form underpinned all his later work.*

Studying the Human Body

Like other Renaissance artists, Michelangelo studied the body in many different ways. One method was to dissect the corpses of dead people so that he could understand how their bones and muscles actually worked. Although Michelangelo did this, he was a little uneasy about it because of his religious beliefs. He also learned about the body by studying ancient Greek and Roman statues and carvings. Live models were less important than they are for modern artists.

◀ *This wooden Crucifix is believed to have been carved by Michelangelo in about 1492 during the time he spent studying at Santo Spirito.*

▶ *Christopher Columbus, born in Genoa, convinced Ferdinand and Isabella of Spain to finance a westward voyage to the Far East. He arrived in the Americas instead.*

The World of 1492

Florence was not alone in experiencing great changes at the time of Lorenzo's death in 1492. Nationalism was growing within Europe as powerful monarchs gained more centralized control of their realms. Spain was reunited as a Catholic monarchy once more under Ferdinand II (1452–1516) and Isabella I (1451–1504), who drove the last Moors (African Muslims) from their country. Most important, Europe gained its first exposure to the New World following the transatlantic voyage of Christopher Columbus (c. 1451–1506) under the Spanish banner. It was a Florentine explorer, Amerigo Vespucci (1454–1512), whose name would be forever linked to the new land, America.

► *The French entry into Florence in 1494 marked a significant change in Italian politics. For much of the sixteenth century, the peninsula was the scene of complicated conflicts involving major European powers.*

Charles VIII Enters Florence

The French King, Charles VIII (1470–98), believed that the Kingdom of Naples was rightfully his. In 1494, he invaded Italy with the intention of capturing Naples. Piero de' Medici (1472–1503) at first opposed the French invasion and then changed his mind, allowing the French safe passage through Florentine territory. His rule collapsed when Pisa took advantage of the presence of French troops to declare its independence. The French arrived in Florence to find the city under a new republican regime.

Savonarola's Florence

The Dominican friar Girolamo Savonarola (1452–98) was a fierce critic of the corruption of the Medici and their followers in Florence. His popularity grew as the political climate in the 1480s and 1490s became more unsettled. When the Medici family fell from power in 1494, at the time of Charles VIII's invasion, Savonarola and his followers gained power. Savonarola imposed an austere rule, suppressing festivals and burning decadent works of art in "bonfires of the vanities." His actions became too extreme for Pope Alexander VI (1431–1503) to tolerate, and in 1497, Savonarola was excommunicated. The following year, he was hanged and then burned.

◄ *This portrait of Girolamo Savonarola by the Florentine painter Fra Bartolomeo (c. 1472–1517) depicts the powerful friar in the austere habit of the Dominican order.*

Michelangelo in Bologna

After stopping briefly in Venice during his flight from Florence, Michelangelo stayed in Bologna for about a year. There he found a patron, Gianfrancesco Aldovrandi, a leading member of Bologna's government and a longtime associate of the Medici family. Aldovrandi helped Michelangelo receive a commission to work on the decoration of the shrine of Saint Dominic. Saint Dominic, the founder of the Dominican order, had died in Bologna in the thirteenth century, and his shrine attracted pilgrims from all over Italy. The three small statues that Michelangelo completed gave an inkling of the power of his later, larger works.

► *This is one of the three works that Michelangelo did in Bologna. The* Angel Bearing a Candlestick *(1494–5) was commissioned for the tomb of St. Dominic. The other statues were of St. Proclus and Bologna's patron saint, St. Petronius, holding a model of the city in his hands.*

1496 Michelangelo leaves Bologna for Rome, where he enjoys the patronage of Cardinal Raffaele Riario and other notables.

c. 1496–8 Michelangelo completes *Bacchus*, his first large-scale sculpture.

1497 He receives a tomb commission for Cardinal Jean Bilheres de Lagraulas, a work that will become the celebrated *Pietà*. Michelangelo visits the Carrara marble quarries for the first time as he searches for material for his sculpture.

c. 1498–9 Michelangelo completes the *Pietà*, establishing himself as one of the foremost artists of his age.

1501 Anxious about the turmoil surrounding Pope Alexander VI and continued French military action, Michelangelo leaves Rome and returns to Florence.

A Tender Masterpiece

Michelangelo was just over twenty-one years old when he first lived in Rome. His love of Florence had not diminished, but conditions there at the height of Savonarola's period in power were still very unsettled. He had already built up a reputation with his works in Bologna, and he knew that he would enjoy the patronage of powerful cardinals and merchants in Rome. Moreover, living in Rome would enable Michelangelo to observe the classical statues that were constantly being unearthed or reexamined. He immersed himself in the study of these ancient celebrations of the human form. The combination of classical inspiration, growing confidence, and wealthy patrons meant that Michelangelo was able to complete his first large works. Chief among these was one of the statues that many people consider his masterpiece, the *Pietà*.

► *The corruption of Alexander VI's papacy distressed many Catholics and almost certainly sowed the seeds for the Protestant Reformation.*

▲ *This map of Rome was drawn in the 1470s. The ancient Roman Colosseum is visible in the center, and the old church of St. Peter's is on the bottom right.*

Alexander VI — the Borgia Pope

Pope Alexander VI was born Rodrigo de Borja (Borgia in Italian) y Doms in Spain in about 1431. His powerful family supported his rise through a succession of Church offices, which led to his being elected pope in 1492. He is remembered for the corruption and violence of his papacy, during which he pursued Borgia family interests and increased the power of the Papal States, Italian territories controlled by the Church. He died in 1503.

Rome in the Renaissance

In the late fifteenth century, Rome was full of the spirit of artistic curiosity that we now term the Renaissance. Like their counterparts in Florence and other Italian cities, artists and scholars in Rome studied ancient art and writing to inspire their celebration of humanity. As the seat of the rich and powerful Catholic Church, the Vatican was able to commission works from Europe's greatest artists. As the heart of the Roman Empire, the city was full of classical ruins and works that could inspire these same artists.

▼ *This ancient Greek statue of a sleeping cupid is one of many that could have inspired Michelangelo.*

▶ *Romans considered Michelangelo's* Bacchus *(1496–7) to be the equal of any ancient statue, which was the highest praise in Renaissance Italy.*

Bacchus

Soon after meeting Michelangelo, Cardinal Riario commissioned him to work on a larger-than-life statue of Bacchus, the ancient Greek god of wine. The statue, Michelangelo's only pagan-inspired major work, gracefully depicts Bacchus raising a goblet of wine while a small satyr (a mythical woodland creature) nibbles the bunch of grapes that Bacchus is holding. The statue was Michelangelo's first large-scale work.

The Sleeping Cupid

One of the first statues completed by Michelangelo in Rome was a *Sleeping Cupid*, which he made for a merchant, Baldassare del Milanese. The work, now lost, resembled a classical statue. The merchant sold it to Cardinal Raffaele Riario (1460–1521) by pretending that it had been found during an archaeological dig. The Cardinal discovered the fraud and recovered his money, but he was curious about the artist and soon welcomed Michelangelo into his influential circle.

◀ *The* Pietà *was the only work that Michelangelo signed.*

The Pietà

Michelangelo was about twenty-five years old when he completed this masterpiece. It shows a very youthful Virgin Mary cradling her son's dead body after he was removed from the cross. Christ's limp, lifeless body contrasts with the quiet strength of Mary's. The work was hailed immediately as a masterpiece.

◀ *Today the* Pietà *(1498–9) is kept in St. Peter's Basilica in Rome, where millions of visitors marvel at its beauty every year.*

A Proud Symbol

1501 Michelangelo receives a commission to complete the sculptural decoration for the Piccolomini altar in Siena's cathedral. He does not honor the contract and produces only four statues for the huge altar.

1503 He is awarded the contract to produce twelve statues of the *Apostles* for Florence Cathedral. Julius II is elected pope.

1504 *David* is completed and wins great acclaim when it is first shown to the public.

Michelangelo never kept himself removed from Pope Alexander VI despite his political intrigues. It became difficult, however, to remain apart from a political climate that was fed by plots, revenge, and grudges. Moreover, Michelangelo's home city, Florence, was reasserting itself as a stable political power that once more (after Savonarola's period in power) valued its artists. In 1501, Michelangelo returned to Florence and was welcomed by the city's new government. Upon arrival, he was given a commission to execute a project that had first been proposed nearly thirty years earlier — to sculpt a huge statue of the biblical hero David. Michelangelo agreed to make the sculpture on the understanding that he would work alone to his own design.

▼ *A sixteenth-century painting by an anonymous artist shows the public burning of Savonarola before the Palazzo della Signoria, the city's seat of government.*

▼ *Each guild had its own emblem, such as this Della Robbia depiction of the Wool Guild.*

The Guilds

Florence had become a wealthy city not because of its military power but because of the success of its merchants and artisans. The powerful Medici family owed its lofty social standing to its prowess in banking. Guilds, associations representing the different crafts and professions, were common in medieval Europe but became especially important in Florence. As well as representing the interests of their own members, guilds gained considerable political power, which was still in effect in Michelangelo's day. There were more than seventy such guilds in Florence. Some had no political power, but others formed alliances to dictate the course of politics in the city and to increase Florentine economic power.

▲ *Machiavelli's diplomatic missions gave him firsthand experience of France, the papacy, and the Holy Roman Emperor.*

Niccolò Machiavelli

Niccolò Machiavelli (1469–1527) revolutionized European thinking with his book on politics, *The Prince* (1513), published five years after his death. Tapping his experience as a Florentine diplomat and military planner, Machiavelli argued that political success is determined by cunning and self-interest rather than by moral duty or religious conviction.

The Florentine Republic

Florence had changed considerably in the seven years since Michelangelo had left it. In 1498, Savonarola had been executed for heresy. The city created a new form of government, the Great Council, in which more than three thousand Florentines had a voice. Florence retained its independence against threats from Piero de' Medici, who wanted to regain control, and Pope Alexander VI's illegitimate son Cesare Borgia (1475–1507). In the complicated political climate, Florence tried to build ties with the French in order to preserve its autonomy.

The David

With *David*, Michelangelo inherited not just a project but a block of marble. Very tall but at the same time shallow, the marble offered a challenge to any sculptor. Florentines considered Michelangelo's success in creating a dynamic yet graceful sculpture from this block of marble to be a huge achievement. David, poised and alert, could symbolize both the republic and the young artist himself. The choice of David, the biblical "underdog," was also important to a city that saw itself constantly threatened by more powerful political rivals.

◄ David *(1501–4). The outsized head and hands defy classical notions of proportion but add to the grandeur of the statue.*

Private Commissions

While working on the *David* and the *Battle of Cascina*, Michelangelo also received commissions from wealthy Florentines who appreciated the artist's genius and were willing to pay for it. Agnolo Doni, Taddeo Taddei, and Bartolommeo Pitti each commissioned a religious tondo (round work of art). Michelangelo's *Doni Tondo* (see page 7) is painted on wood; the others are bas-relief sculptures.

► The Tondo Pitti *(1504–05) depicts the Madonna with Child and the infant Saint John (upper left).*

▼ *This 1542 painting by Bastiano da Sangallo (1481-1551) is a copy of Michelangelo's cartoon (rough draft) of the* Battle of Cascina.

The Battle of Cascina

In 1503, Florence turned to one of its greatest sons, Leonardo da Vinci, to paint a huge historical mural for the Palazzo Vecchio. Leonardo chose the Battle of Anghiari, fought against the Milanese in 1440, as his theme, but he failed to finish the project. Michelangelo was then offered a similar commission and chose to depict the Florentine victory over the Pisans at Cascina in 1364. Like Leonardo's work, Michelangelo's mural was never completed.

Missed Opportunities

1505 Michelangelo is summoned to Rome by Pope Julius II. The pope commissions Michelangelo to create a massive sculpted tomb. Michelangelo spends nearly a year in Carrara choosing marble for the project, but the pope changes his mind about going ahead.
1506 Michelangelo is present when the Romans rediscover the ancient *Laocoön group* sculpture. He begins work in Bologna on a bronze statue of Julius II. He completes the *Bruges Madonna* sculpture commissioned by the Mouscron brothers, Flemish cloth merchants. It is the first of his works to leave the Italian peninsula. Pope Julius II first proposes that Michelangelo paint the ceiling of the Sistine Chapel in the Vatican.
1508 The bronze statue of Julius II is completed, but it is destroyed by the Bolognese in 1511.

After the triumphs of the *Pietà* and the *David*, Michelangelo entered a period of missed opportunities. The papacy of Julius II (1443–1513) was in marked contrast to that of Alexander VI, and the new pope was destined to become one of history's greatest artistic patrons. Summoned to Rome in 1505 by the new pope, Michelangelo abandoned plans to sculpt twelve *Apostles* in Florence. The pope's huge commission for Michelangelo, a massive sculpted tomb, was also destined to be abandoned. Michelangelo's bronze papal statue was to be destroyed in 1511. Despite these false starts, the artistic relationship between the pope and the artist united two of the most headstrong characters of sixteenth-century Italy.

An Unfinished Project
Michelangelo had just begun to sculpt the twelve *Apostles* for Florence Cathedral when he was summoned to Rome by Pope Julius II in 1505. The pope had in mind a far more ambitious project — a huge sculpted tomb for the new St. Peter's Basilica. In 1506, Michelangelo set off for the famous marble quarries at Carrara. He spent nearly a year choosing materials before the pope changed his mind and abandoned the project. The time was not lost, however. Michelangelo gained even more knowledge of stone, an abiding love since his childhood.

▼ *The* Laocoön group *was completed by three artists in the first century* B.C. *and originally stood on the Greek island of Rhodes.*

A Rediscovered Treasure
In 1506, Michelangelo was present when an ancient Greek sculptural masterpiece, the *Laocoön group*, was uncovered in the garden of a former palace of Emperor Nero in Rome. The mastery of this work inspired Michelangelo, and he made sketches of the sculpture from memory in later years.

▲ *The unfinished* St. Matthew *(c. 1505–6), now on display in the Galleria dell'Accademia in Florence, is all that Michelangelo completed of his intended collection of twelve* Apostles.

Pope Julius II

The Borgia pope, Alexander VI, had died in 1503. His successor, Pius III (c. 1439–1503), died soon after becoming pope. The next pope, Julius II, aimed to restore the papacy and save Italy from being destroyed by secret political schemes. He increased the power of the Papal States and curbed the influence of France in Italy. He is best remembered, though, for his artistic patronage. His plans for a massive sculpted tomb drew him towards Michelangelo, but he also recognized the genius of artists such as Donato Bramante (c. 1444–1514) and Raphael (1483–1520).

▼ *This is part of the early plans Michelangelo drew up for the enormous tomb for Pope Julius II sometime after receiving the commission in 1505. His plans combined classical architecture with dramatic sculptures.*

▶ *Portrait of Pope Julius II (1511–12) by Raphael. The papacy of Julius II lasted only ten years, but during that time, he promoted Italian stability and greatly strengthened the office he held.*

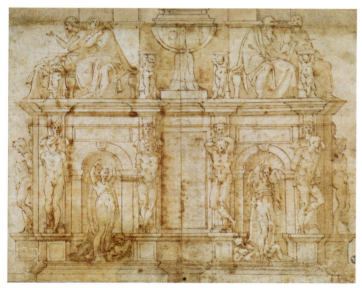

The New St. Peter's

Pope Julius II was an ambitious patron of the arts. In about 1506, he commissioned the architect Donato Bramante to demolish the original St. Peter's Basilica and replace it with a Renaissance masterpiece. The pope's planned tomb was to be a feature of the new St. Peter's, along with works by Raphael and other artists.

▶ *This medallion was cast to commemorate the founding of the new St. Peter's Basilica in about 1506. The basilica eventually looked very different from this image.*

▼ *Carrara stone workers in the late sixteenth century used some of the same skills and tools that quarrymen used during Michelangelo's time there in about 1506.*

The Marble Quarries

Having received his commission to design and construct the papal tomb, Michelangelo set off for the marble quarries near the city of Carrara in Tuscany. These quarries had — and retain to this day — the reputation for being the source of some of the finest marble in the world. Michelangelo spent eight months examining the rock and studying how the quarrymen retrieved the best pieces without damaging them. Although the tomb project was postponed, Michelangelo developed an even more profound awareness of how to work with marble.

The Sistine Ceiling

1508 Michelangelo begins work on the ceiling frescoes.
1510 With half the frescoes finished, Michelangelo takes a short break.
1512 The Sistine Chapel ceiling is completed, and its frescoes are unveiled to the public on November 1, All Saint's Day. Michelangelo returns to Florence for a short stay.

In early 1508, Pope Julius II set Michelangelo the task of painting the ceiling of the most important chapel in the Vatican, the Sistine Chapel. Various painters had been working on the walls since 1481, but the ceiling decoration was confined to painted stars. The pope wanted something much more dramatic. Michelangelo viewed himself primarily as a sculptor, so a painting project on such a scale — and in such a setting — was a supreme challenge. It took Michelangelo four years to paint the 10,000 square feet (930 square meters) of the ceiling, but the result was another triumph.

The Sistine Chapel

The Sistine Chapel, where the most sacred rituals took place and where popes were elected, was named after Julius II's uncle, Pope Sixtus IV. From an artistic point of view, the chapel and its adjoining rooms would form the master stroke of Julius II's plans for the Vatican.

▲ Portrait of Sixtus IV *in a detail of a fresco by Melozzo da Forlì (1438–94).*

► *The* Sybil of Delphi *is one of the seven Prophets and five Sybils (pagan seers) portrayed on both sides of the central part of the ceiling.*

The Creation of Adam

The most famous scene on the ceiling of the Sistine Chapel, *The Creation of Adam*, occupies a central position on the vault. The two main figures — God and Adam — take their potency from the way Michelangelo depicted their bodies, which twist like spirals. Their shoulders wheel in the opposite direction of their legs. God, who reaches out to bring Adam to life, is surrounded by a cloud of angels.

▼ The Creation of Adam *(c. 1508-12). Some scholars argue that the woman encircled by God's left arm is Eve.*

The Sistine Ceiling

▼ *A fresco from the cycle* Scenes from the Life of Moses *(1481–2) by Sandro Botticelli. As one of Florence's leading fifteenth-century artists, Botticelli added his characteristic lightness of touch to this fresco.*

The Wall Frescoes

Before Michelangelo got involved with the Sistine Chapel, a number of other leading artists had decorated the lower walls with frescoes. Botticelli, Ghirlandaio, Perugino, Signorelli, and others painted scenes from the life of Moses on one wall and episodes from the life of Christ on the other wall across the chapel.

Michelangelo at Work

Michelangelo's work on the Sistine Chapel ceiling helped establish his reputation as a "lone genius." He refused to use the scaffolding that Bramante, the pope's Vatican architect, had erected, and he also refused the assistance of experienced fresco painters who had been brought from Florence to offer advice. Michelangelo locked himself in the chapel with just a couple of workmen. The scaffolding he had designed got him to the proper height without support from either ceiling or walls. Lying on his back, with his head propped on a stool, he painted the ceiling above him.

▼ *In a letter dated 1509 addressed to his brother, Buonarroto Buonarotti, Michelangelo wrote: "Here I am with many worries and with very great fatigue of body, and I do not have friends of any kind nor do I want any, and I do not have enough time to eat."*

The Ceiling Decoration

Michelangelo intended the ceiling to be a celebration of humanity before the coming of Christ. The nine central panels from the Old Testament depict (1) the Separation of Light from Darkness, (2) the Creation of Planets, Sun, Moon, and Stars, (3) the Separation of Land and Sea, (4) the Creation of Adam, (5) the Creation of Eve, (6) the Fall and Expulsion from Paradise, (7) the Sacrifice of Noah, (8) the Flood, and (9) the Drunkenness of Noah. These panels are flanked by panels of Prophets and Sibyls (10). The vaulting cells between these panels depict the Ancestors of Christ (11). The four pendentives show scenes of salvation of the Israelites from the *Old Testament* (12). Other Ancestors of Christ are depicted in the lunettes (13).

▲ *A painstaking renovation program in the 1980s restored the vividness to Michelangelo's* Sistine Chapel *ceiling painting, allowing viewers to marvel at the boldness of his colors.*

Adjoining Geniuses

1508 Raphael is commissioned to decorate the suite of rooms adjoining the Sistine Chapel. He continues to work on the apartments until his death in 1520, after which his assistants take over the task. Once work begins on the Sistine Chapel ceiling, Michelangelo and Raphael find themselves working within feet of each other for four years.

Pope Julius II lived up to his reputation as a creative patron of the arts in his choice of artists to decorate the Vatican. Even before he had convinced Michelangelo to work on the Sistine Chapel ceiling, the pope had commissioned Raphael to work on the private apartments adjoining the chapel. Raphael was eight years younger than Michelangelo but had already established himself as one of Italy's leading painters. The commission offered him the chance to display the full range of his talents. In the competitive atmosphere of early sixteenth-century Rome, many observers were prepared to see the Vatican decoration as a battle between two geniuses.

▲ A sculptor's chisels and sandstone, rather than paints and brushes, were Michelangelo's preferred tools.

▶ Leon Battista Alberti used his immense knowledge of mathematics to conduct systematic studies of art and architecture.

Michelangelo, Sculptor in Rome

Throughout his life, Michelangelo considered himself to be a sculptor rather than a painter. Even during the time he spent working on the Sistine ceiling, he signed his letters "Michelangelo, sculptor in Rome." Many people believe he took on the job simply to keep alive his preferred project, the pope's huge sculpted tomb.

▼ Michelangelo's supposed self-portrait (right) features in his fresco of the Old Testament figures Azor and Sadoc in this lunette of the Sistine Chapel.

Artist vs. Craftsman

One of the many new ideas that developed during the Renaissance concerned the nature of artists. Medieval artists were considered craftsmen, just as we might describe plasterers or furniture makers. We know little of the artists whose work fills most European cathedrals. Even Michelangelo's father, disapproving of his son's ambitions, described artists as "workers" who had a poor social standing. Attitudes changed in the fifteenth century, influenced by the writings of the scholar Leon Battista Alberti (1404–72). His treatise *On Painting* (1436) claimed that artists are among the "most noble and wonderful minds." The notion of artistic identity began to take root.

AZOR

SADOCH

▶ *Raphael's* School of Athens *(c. 1509–11) in the Stanza della Segnatura features a dialogue between Plato and Aristotle (center left and right) surrounded by other great philosophers.*

Painting after Michelangelo's Sistine Ceiling

There is no doubt that Michelangelo and Raphael felt the need to match each other's accomplishments in the Vatican. Michelangelo reluctantly took on the Sistine commission after being taunted that by refusing, he was acknowledging Raphael's superiority. Raphael, in turn, acknowledged Michelangelo's importance by adopting some of his techniques and by including a portrait of him in his own work.

▶ *This detail from the foreground of the* School of Athens *shows Heraclitus as a likeness of Michelangelo.*

◀ Self-Portrait *(c. 1506) by Raphael. Although he learned a lot from Leonardo's and Michelangelo's work, Raphael developed his own style with harmonious compositions and dynamic figures.*

Raphael

Raffaello Sanzio, or Raphael (1483–1520) trained in Perugia and then in Florence. He was an established artist by his early twenties. In 1508, he was commissioned to decorate the papal apartments next to the Sistine Chapel. His frescoes linked classical learning (with depictions of philosophers such as Aristotle and Plato of ancient Greece) with Christian themes. Raphael assumed more responsibilities after the death of Pope Julius II in 1513 and found less time to paint. He had completed only two of the four apartments at the time of his death.

▲ *A workshop's patron often supervised the painting process, dictating the composition as well as the choice of colors for a fresco.*

The Art of Fresco Painting

The walls of many Renaissance churches and homes were decorated with paintings executed on freshly laid lime plaster. Such a painting is known as a fresco, from the Italian for "fresh." The sinopia, a preliminary drawing made with reddish pigment, was made in a layer of plaster, then each day a small area was covered with a fine layer of wet intonaco (plaster). Artists painted onto this. The colors penetrated the plaster and became a part of the wall. The artist needed to know exactly how much paint the plaster would absorb. Adding too much paint would cause the plaster to "rot," ruining an entire section. Michelangelo, working on the Sistine Chapel ceiling, faced all these difficulties while working on his back and painting above himself.

Return to Stone

1513 A second contract for Pope Julius II's tomb is drawn up. Michelangelo begins two statues of *Slaves* and a huge seated sculpture of *Moses*, which becomes the only element of the original plans to feature in the finished tomb. Michelangelo buys a house in Macel' de' Corvi in Rome.

1514 Michelangelo signs a contract for the *Risen Christ* sculpture for the church of St. Maria Sopra Minerva in Rome. When a black vein in the marble appears in the area of the face, he abandons this first version.

1516 The second in a series of modified plans sees a general scaling down of the tomb's scale. Projects planned by Julius II's papal successors keep Michelangelo from working on the tomb.

Pope Julius II died in 1513, just a year after Michelangelo's work on the Sistine Chapel ceiling was completed. Although the pope had died, his original project for Michelangelo — the massive papal tomb — lived on. Michelangelo returned to his great love, working with stone, and began work on the tomb. The project did not continue smoothly. Ascanio Condivi (1525–74), Michelangelo's biographer, later wrote that "Michelangelo again embarked upon the tragedy of the tomb." The tomb attained this tragic reputation because of all the twists and turns in its planning and execution. It took forty years for the tomb to progress from its original designs in 1505 to its completion in 1545. By then it was a mere shadow of Michelangelo's original ambitious plan.

Victories and Slaves

Soon after the death of Pope Julius II, his heirs recommissioned Michelangelo to work on a modified version of the papal tomb. The collective theme of the tomb's thirty-two large statues was the triumph of the Catholic Church over the pagan world. The lower register would contain representations of *Victories* (representing the provinces converted under Julius II) and *Slaves* (representing pagan peoples acknowledging the Catholic faith). Above would be statues of *Moses* and *St. Paul*, representing the triumph of mind over body. Michelangelo cherished these plans but saw them change under successive popes while he himself worked on other projects in between.

▶ The Bound Slave *(1513–15) was one of the statues intended to symbolize pagan converts to Catholicism. It, along with many others, was not included in the completed tomb and is now in the Louvre Museum in Paris.*

The Reformation

◀ *In 1517, Martin Luther nailed a list of ninety-five theses (topics for debate) to the door of the castle church in Wittenberg, protesting the Church system of indulgences and triggering the movement known as the Reformation.*

Excesses within the Catholic Church led to a powerful reaction known as the Reformation in the early sixteenth century. The leading force was Martin Luther (1483–1546), a German monk. Luther visited Rome in 1510 and was shocked by the irreligious behavior of the senior clergy. His opinions became stronger in 1517 when the Church began selling indulgences, which supposedly cleared people's paths to heaven, to pay for the rebuilding of St. Peter's. Luther publicized his concerns about corruption, calling for a reform of the Church. The newly invented printing press spread Luther's wider message that salvation depends more on biblical study than priestly intervention. By the 1520s, many Europeans called themselves "Protestants" because they were protesting against the wrongs of Rome.

Pope Leo X

Pope Leo X (1475–1521) was the second son of Lorenzo de' Medici, who in effect ruled Florence during its most glorious Renaissance period. This background ensured that Giovanni de' Medici (Leo X's original name) received an exceptional education and became familiar with Florence's leading artists and thinkers. With the fall of the Medici in 1494, he traveled through Northern Europe, but by the time of his election as pope (in 1513), the family had returned to power. Leo X combined his role of pope with that of Florentine ruler until his death in 1521.

▼ *Portrait of Leo X (c. 1518) by Raphael. This portrait captures the sense of self-possession and confidence that the pope displayed.*

The Finished Tomb

Despite the changes and interruptions that overshadowed Julius II's tomb, Michelangelo always cherished the project. He completed some of his most majestic sculpture while working on the tomb, even if the finished works did not always survive the changes in overall design. Sometimes despairing of the chance ever to complete the project, Michelangelo received the commission to complete the tomb in 1542. By then, plans had been abandoned to place the tomb in St. Peter's Basilica. The completed tomb was finally unveiled in Rome's church of San Pietro in Vincoli, Rome, in 1545.

▶ *The central seated figure of* Moses *(1513–c. 1516) is all that remains of Michelangelo's original plans for the tomb of Pope Julius II.*

The Evolving Plans

Michelangelo's original plans for Julius II's tomb had been agreed upon with the pope himself, and they reflected the ambitions of both powerful men. Following Julius II's death, however, the plans underwent a number of changes, each time representing a more modest tomb. A series of other papal commissions robbed Michelangelo of the time needed to complete even these scaled-down plans.

▼ *The illustrations show the diminishing scale of Julius's tomb, as seen in the plans from 1505 (left), 1513 (center), and 1516 (right).*

1516 Michelangelo is contracted to build a façade for the church of San Lorenzo in Florence.
1517 Returning to Florence, Michelangelo begins work on the façade plans.
1520 Pope Leo X and other Medici commission Michelangelo to build a New Sacristy in San Lorenzo to house a family mausoleum.
1520 Michelangelo begins work on the New Sacristy with a three-year break while the Medici are removed from power (1527–30).

The Book of the Courtier

Baldassare Castiglione (1478–1529) was an Italian diplomat and writer who had served in many of the great courts of Italy and Spain. Just as Machiavelli had used similar experience to develop his political theories, Castiglione used his observations of courtly life to devise a code of behavior for the ideal courtier. His most famous work, which was widely translated throughout Europe, was *The Book of the Courtier* (1528). Quite apart from its guidelines for aristocratic manners, the book provides a firsthand account of courtly life in the sixteenth century. One of its characters is Giuliano de' Medici, youngest son of Lorenzo de' Medici and brother of Pope Leo X.

▶ Portrait of Castiglione *(1516) by Raphael. Castiglione proposed the notion of a cultured nobleman whom he considered the ideal courtier.*

Summoned Back to Florence

The Medici family, which had provided Michelangelo with vital early support and patronage, once more figured largely in his artistic career. Pope Leo X, the son of Lorenzo de' Medici and Michelangelo's patron, provided the artist with a direct link to his own past. Beginning in 1516, Leo X and his cousin Cardinal de' Medici (the future Pope Clement VII) engaged Michelangelo in a series of important projects that would commemorate their own family.

▼ Leo X Entering Florence *(1550) by Giorgio Vasari. Leo X, a Medici, triumphantly entered Florence soon after becoming pope in 1513.*

▲ *This wooden model, based on Michelangelo's design for San Lorenzo's façade, showed how doors, windows, and sculpted details blended harmoniously into an overall composition.*

The Façade of San Lorenzo

Pope Leo X preferred employing Michelangelo's artistic genius to glorify the Medici family in Florence rather than decorating the Vatican in Rome. Impressed by Michelangelo's architectural designs for Julius II's tomb, he summoned the artist to Florence to design a new façade and family mausoleum at the church of San Lorenzo. The façade was never built, but Michelangelo's designs showed how he was beginning to use architectural features such as bays, portals, and columns as artistic features in their own right rather than simply as background for statues.

The Return of the Medici

The invasion of Italy by French troops in 1494 forced Piero de' Medici to leave Florence (see page 13). Exiled from their own city, the Medici watched as Savonarola's rule was replaced by the republic led by Piero Soderini (1452—1522) in 1502. The Medici then turned to another European power, Spain, to reassert themselves. With the help of a Spanish defeat of the Florentine army in 1512, the Medici returned to rule Florence. Two of Lorenzo de' Medici's sons — Giovanni (later Pope Leo X) and Giuliano — were aided by their cousin Giulio (later Pope Clement VII) and their nephew Lorenzo (1492–1519) in reasserting Medici control.

▲ *The New Sacristy, San Lorenzo. Michelangelo's designs, inspired by his great predecessor Brunelleschi, used the walls as organic parts of the design rather than as inert planes waiting to be filled with statues and ornaments.*

The New Sacristy

In 1520, Michelangelo abandoned the San Lorenzo façade to work on another Medici project, the New Sacristy, for the same church. The Medici wanted a mausoleum to contain monuments to four prominent family members. Michelangelo developed his architectural style even further, imposing a stark and severe beauty. He worked on it until 1534 with a break from 1527 to 1530 when the Medici had again been expelled from Florence. Now known as one of the Medici Chapels, it contains only two finished tombs.

▲ *Two statues, representing* Dusk *and* Dawn, *flank the tomb of Lorenzo de' Medici.*

Today, the handsome church of San Lorenzo still has a blank wall where Michelangelo's façade would have been.

A dome covers the New Sacristy at the church's western end.

San Lorenzo

San Lorenzo occupies the site of the earliest church in Florence. Cosimo the Elder (1389–1464), who established Medici dominance in Florence, had built a splendid residence near it in the fifteenth century, making San Lorenzo the parish church of the Medici family. It was designed by the Florentine architect Filippo Brunelleschi (1377–1446), who rediscovered the long-lost principles of linear perspective in the early fifteenth century. Cosimo's successors considered the church to be the best showcase for Medici glory.

Breakthroughs in Architecture

c. 1524 Pope Clement VII commissions Michelangelo to build the Medici Library in the San Lorenzo complex.
1524 Michelangelo's plans for the Medici Library are approved, and building commences while work continues on the Medici Tombs.
1527 Rome is sacked by a mob of undisciplined soldiers in the pay of Holy Roman Emperor Charles V. Florentines take advantage of the pope's weakened position to expel the Medici and declare a new republic. Michelangelo stops working on the Medici projects.
1529 Michelangelo takes charge of the republican fortifications against the besieging forces of Charles V.
1530 The republican forces are defeated, and the Medici return to power in Florence. Michelangelo resumes work on Medici architectural projects.

Michelangelo constantly adapted ideas from abandoned or postponed works and put them to use in new settings. Having begun work on the Medici tombs in San Lorenzo, he was called to mastermind another Medici project — an imposing new library to house the family's substantial collection of documents. Here he took his ideas on architectural harmony a stage further, tapping ideas he had developed on both the New Sacristy and the long-delayed tomb for Julius II.

Mannerist Architecture

Michelangelo explored all the possibilities of crafting stone to the best effect. He took the classical ideals of proportion and harmony and applied them to an entire building rather than simply considering it as a backdrop for beautiful statues and other decorations. He was one of the first architects to introduce Mannerist ideas (see page 32) to his work by deliberately misleading the eye and by altering perspective. Ideas from his abandoned projects resurfaced, sometimes decades later, in his work in Florence and Rome.

▲ *An armillary sphere (globe) in the Medici Library shows the equator and lines of the tropics.*

The Medici Library

While Michelangelo was involved with the Medici tombs in San Lorenzo, he was commissioned to build a library in the same church complex, above a row of monastic cells on the ground floor. The books had been collected by Lorenzo de' Medici, and the library is also called the Laurentian Library as a result. Only a noble family as powerful as the Medici could have amassed such an array of manuscripts. The ambitious new building to house them represented another element in the process of turning San Lorenzo into a Medici showpiece.

◀ *The triple staircase leading up to the library became a feature in itself, occupying more than half of the entrance room.*

▶ *The Reading Room of the Medici Library. The handsome rows of desks, flanking a central aisle, continue the three-part nature of the staircase leading to the room.*

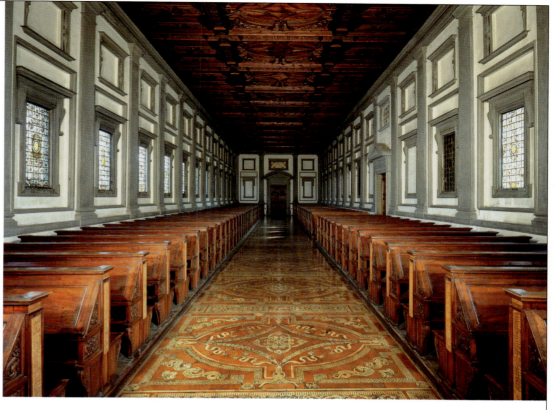

The Reading Room

The Reading Room provided the main function of the Medici Library — to house documents and to allow people the chance to read them. The desks and ceiling panels were completed by other craftsmen, but they conform to Michelangelo's original designs. The room is deliberately restrained, compared with the library entrance, so that people are distracted from the real treasures — the documents themselves.

The Medici Republic

Pope Clement VII (Giulio de' Medici) had formed an alliance with Holy Roman Emperor Charles V (1500–58), who was also king of Spain. Charles V's troops besieged Florence in 1530, eventually gaining control of the city. The Florentine Republic remained in name only, with Alessandro de' Medici (c. 1511–37) becoming its leader in 1531 and governor for life a year later. Hereditary power rested with the Medici as Florence later became the capital of the Grand Duchy of Tuscany, but the city no longer enjoyed its former power or autonomy.

▶ *Michelangelo's plans for the fortifications of the Porta al Prato di Ognissanti (c. 1529) show his reliance on acute defensive angles.*

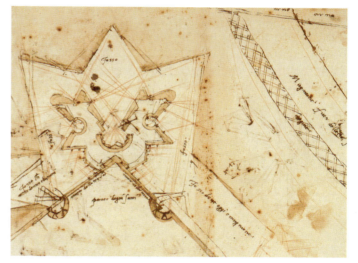

▼ *During the siege of Florence, Michelangelo saved the bell tower of the church of San Miniato al Monte by covering it with mattresses.*

▲ Portrait of Alessandro de' Medici (c. 1534) by Vasari. He had Michelangelo pay a fine for his republican involvement before having him resume various Medici projects.

Michelangelo's Fortifications

Rome was sacked in 1527, forcing Pope Clement VII, a Medici, to loosen his grip on Florence. The Florentines revolted, expelling the Medici rulers, and reestablished a republic. Three years later, the Medici besieged Florence, and Michelangelo designed the city's fortifications. He showed an awareness of the importance of new weapons such as cannons, and the defensive structures offered a minimum of exposed targets for attacking artillery. Low walls, hugging the hillsides surrounding Florence, also jutted out at acute angles to allow defenders to counterattack.

The Last Judgment

Growing unhappy with the increasingly autocratic rule of the Medici, Michelangelo left Florence in 1534 and returned to Rome, where he would live for the rest of his life. The Medici control in Rome had ended with the death of Pope Clement VII that same year, and Michelangelo immediately obtained a commission with the new pope, Paul III (1468–1549). The result would be another towering masterpiece, *The Last Judgment*, filling the enormous altar wall of the Sistine Chapel.

The Fresco Program

Michelangelo abandoned typical Italian representations of a seated, bearded Christ in his depiction of *The Last Judgment*. (See pages 34-35.) The fresco comprises three main bands of figures, each group subdivided into smaller ones. At the top is the Court of Heaven, with a striding Christ flanked by the Virgin and a host of the elect. Below them are the angels with the trumpets of the Last Judgment, with souls rising to Heaven (left) or plunging to damnation (right). The bottom row features the resurrection of the dead (left) and Charon ferrying the souls of the damned to Hell (right).

▶ *A damned soul has a look of despair as demons pull him to Hell in this middle-register detail of* The Last Judgment.

A New Style of Painting

By about 1520, roughly a century after the first great works of the Renaissance, artists began to abandon their adherence to the principles of harmony, composition, and balance established during the preceding century. Instead they introduced exaggerated detail, artificial color, and strange distortions of perspective. Art historians use the term "Mannerism" (from the Italian *maniera*, meaning "style" or "stylishness") to describe this trend, which lasted from roughly 1520 to 1600. Michelangelo's figures in the Sistine Chapel, with their powerful bodies and movement, were an important reference for the Mannerist painters. Some critics have seen Mannerism as a reflection of the instability of the period, with its constant warfare and the upheaval of the Reformation.

The Sack of Rome

The political chaos that had become a feature of Italian life in the late fifteenth century became even more alarming by the 1520s. Rival European powers fought over the Italian peninsula, which had not been united since the time of the Roman Empire. The two main protagonists were France and Spain. The Spanish king was also the Holy Roman Emperor Charles V. In 1527, his army in Italy became mutinous because soldiers had not been paid. They ran out of control and attacked Rome, an evil city in the eyes of the many German Lutherans in the army. The destruction lasted for weeks, leaving buildings and priceless art objects destroyed.

▼ *Rioting soldiers attacked Castel Sant'Angelo, the pope's stronghold, holding him prisoner during the Sack of Rome in 1527.*

▲ *The complicated, artificial postures of the group, along with the use of unnatural colors in Jacobo Pontormo's* Deposition *(1526–8), typify the Mannerist approach to painting.*

▲ *Charles V had been sovereign of the Netherlands, Austria, Germany, half of Italy, Spain, parts of eastern France, North Africa, and a growing American empire. Exhausted by threats from all sides, he abdicated in 1555-6, dividing his lands between his brother and son.*

Charles V

Emperor Charles V had inherited the realms of Spain, where he reigned as Charles I, and the Holy Roman Empire while he was still in his late teens. Together, they provided Charles V with an enormous territory, especially in Spain's growing American empire. Charles V faced threats from all sides. France was a growing rival, and the Turks threatened the heartland of the Holy Roman Empire in Central Europe. Moreover, the German core of the Empire was being torn apart as princes and noblemen joined the Lutheran cause.

Pope Paul III

Clement VII's successor, Pope Paul III, was a member of the Farnese family, and his artistic ambitions matched those of Clement VII. Pope Paul III had marveled at Michelangelo's Sistine Chapel ceiling and commissioned Michelangelo to execute Clement VII's plans to decorate the huge wall behind the chapel altar. The theme agreed on by Clement VII and Michelangelo — *The Last Judgment* — was significant because it represented a response to the divisions affecting Christianity in the early days of the Reformation. Michelangelo worked on the enormous fresco constantly from 1536 to 1541.

◀ The Last Judgment *replaced fifteenth-century frescoes by Perugino as well as Michelangelo's own two semicircular lunettes, painted at the same time as the ceiling.*

▶ *A detail from* The Last Judgment. *Scholars have suggested that the face in the flayed skin of St. Bartholomew is that of Michelangelo himself.*

1534 Paul III sets about reforming the Catholic Church (the Counter-Reformation) as a response to the Reformation during his fifteen-year papacy.
1536 Michelangelo meets the poet Vittoria Colonna.
1540 The Society of Jesus (the Jesuit Order) is founded, with Ignatius Loyola (1491–1556) as its leader.
1543 *The Index* (of banned books) is established as part of the Counter-Reformation. Copernicus' work on planetary motion is published.
1545–63 The first session of The Council of Trent meets to strengthen Catholic dogma and doctrine.
c. 1564 Parts of Michelangelo's nude figures in the Sistine Chapel are covered.

Spiritual Struggles

The last decades of Michelangelo's life before his death in 1564 constituted a time of turmoil and new thinking. The political life of Italy remained unsettled, with constant conflict and shifting alliances. Even more unsettling was the profound change in the way people thought. The Reformation, aided by the development of the printing press, had allowed Europeans to question and quit the Catholic Church. In response, Rome had to rethink its own position on nearly every aspect of doctrine and ritual. The result was the Counter-Reformation, which signaled a strengthened and aggressive new approach to Catholic leadership. But the Church was set to face conflict in another arena — scientific theory that questioned Catholic teaching.

▲ *Martin Luther's powerful and persuasive preaching in Germany led many Europeans to question and later abandon the Catholic Church.*

Pope Paul III and the Counter-Reformation

The Reformation, which had been set in motion by Martin Luther in Germany, attracted converts across much of northern and central Europe. Many Catholics echoed some of the Protestant complaints, especially the charge that senior Catholic Church leaders in Rome led worldly and corrupt lives that were far removed from the Christian ideals of purity and humility, not to mention poverty. Pope Paul III addressed these concerns and set in motion what we now term the Counter-Reformation. The pope appointed capable leaders to the senior ranks of the church to help Rome win back many of the Christians who had been lost to the Protestants. In 1540, he approved the formation of the Society of Jesus (Jesuits), who would use persuasion and guile to win back believers.

▲ *This image from the church Il Gesù in Rome depicts Pope Paul III receiving Ignatius Loyola, the Jesuit founder who strove to be what he called a "soldier of Christ."*

Council of Trent

The Catholic Church set about remedying some of the worst excesses targeted by Luther and other Protestants. Abuses of relics, monastic corruption, and the sale of indulgences were countered in an effort to give the Church more vigor. On the subject of doctrine, however, the Church stood firm and reasserted many of its beliefs at the Council of Trent, which met in three sessions between 1545 and 1563. Rather than try to find a common ground to work out a compromise with the Protestants, the Church used the Council to strengthen its own doctrines and to attack some of Luther's — notably his belief that individuals can achieve salvation by faith alone, without the help of priests.

▲ *The Council of Trent strengthened the Catholic Church but made the Christian division irreversible.*

Vittoria Colonna

Poetry was prized as an art form in the Renaissance. Verses were written by popes and monarchs, nuns and priests, artists and servants. Michelangelo composed many sonnets, commenting on events in his own life and celebrating beauty, usually male. He did, however, have a deeply spiritual relationship with a female poet, Vittoria Colonna (1492–1547), whose friendship he valued greatly. Michelangelo was with her at her deathbed in 1547 and later composed a touching sonnet commemorating her.

▶ *A medallion with Colonna's portrait indicates the level of respect she attained among the Italian artistic world in the sixteenth century.*

Religion and Art

Imbued with the spirit of the Counter-Reformation, the Catholic Church began to reconsider religious art in the second half of the sixteenth century. Paintings and sculpture were now intended to be more than simply devotional works — they had to act as propaganda that could elicit profound emotional responses. The distortions and vivid colors of Mannerist works served this purpose neatly, and after 1600, artists plunged even deeper into the world of the spectacular in what is called the Baroque style.

▶ *A detail of* The Conversion of St. Paul *(c. 1542–5), part of Michelangelo's last fresco cycle, painted in the Pauline Chapel in the Vatican when he was sixty-seven.*

Copernicus' Theory

Michelangelo's last decades saw scientific changes that would rock previous certainties almost as much as the Reformation. As well as looking back to ancient Greece and Rome for artistic inspiration, the Renaissance triggered a thirst for knowledge and scientific inquiry.

Throughout the Middle Ages, Europeans satisfied themselves with the Church's teaching that Earth — and by extension mankind — was the center of the Universe and that everything else moved around it. In about 1514, a Polish monk named Nicolaus Copernicus (1473–1543) used mathematics and astronomical study to propose that Earth and other planets revolved around the Sun. Fearing controversy, he refused to publish his findings until he neared death.

▲ *Copernicus' book,* On the Revolution of Heavenly Bodies *(1543), shook the Western world and had a profound influence on the development of science.*

An Architect of Rome

Michelangelo's reputation as a bold and gifted architect had been established with the Medici projects that were well under way when he left Florence for Rome in 1534. The Rome he reentered was bursting with architectural projects, part of the Catholic Church's reassertion of its power and grandeur. Often competing with established architects such as the Sangallo family, Michelangelo received a series of important commissions.

1538 Work begins on Michelangelo's redesigned Campidoglio (Capitoline Hill project).
c. 1540 Michelangelo carves the famous bust of *Brutus.*
1542 A contract concluded with Julius II's heirs leads to the final stage of the long-delayed tomb project. Michelangelo also begins work on frescoes for a new Pauline Chapel in the Vatican.
1545 The tomb of Julius II is completed.
1546 Michelangelo takes over the design of the Palazzo Farnese, completing the building with a bold Mannerist flourish.

The Brutus Commission

Michelangelo's bust of *Brutus* (one of Julius Caesar's chief assassins) was completed in 1540. The work, Michelangelo's last work with political significance, was commissioned by Cardinal Niccolò Ridolfi, who had fled Florence for Rome in 1530, when the Medici return to power put an end to Florentine republican ideals. The work imbues Brutus with a compelling mixture of determination, energy, and contempt. These attributes led Brutus to murder when Caesar became too dictatorial. Michelangelo was no doubt comparing the target of Brutus's scorn with the overpowerful Medici family in Florence.

◄ *The* Brutus *(1540) is almost certainly an idealized portrait of Michelangelo's patron, Cardinal Niccolò Ridolfi.*

► Portrait of Poggio Braccriolini *(1380–1459) from a fifteenth-century manuscript. In about 1414, he discovered the manuscript of Vitruvius.*

Ancient Roman Models

Architects in Rome needed to look no farther than their home city to derive inspiration. Ancient Roman buildings and ruins provided models and practical teaching aids for re-creating the classical ideals of harmony and proportion.

► *The seemingly unsupported great dome of the Pantheon (A.D. 118–28) in central Rome inspired many Renaissance architects.*

Vitruvius' Proportions

Italian Renaissance architects derived much of their knowledge of classical buildings from the works of Marcus Vitruvius (active 46–30 B.C.). An ardent admirer of classical Greek architecture in particular, Vitruvius wrote the definitive text *On Architecture (De architectura)*. The work, divided into ten books dealing with all types of public building, emphasized the importance of proportion and harmony, underpinning the ideals of the Renaissance more than fourteen hundred years after Vitruvius' death.

Palazzo Farnese

Michelangelo took over the design and building of the imposing Palazzo Farnese when the original architect, Antonio da Sangallo the Younger (c. 1485–1546) died. Sangallo had completed the first two floors in classical style. Michelangelo, anticipating later Mannerist architecture, gave the upper floor larger windows and higher ceilings — reversing the accepted practice of giving upper floors less importance. This reversal introduces tension into the way we perceive the building.

▶ *A colossal head of the Emperor Constantine (c. 330) is one of the treasures of the museums in the Campidoglio.*

▲ *Palazzo Farnese, Rome. Behind the restrained classical façade is a lavishly furnished and decorated interior.*

▶ *The second-century* A.D. *statue of Marcus Aurelius, with the pedestal by Michelangelo, was placed in the center of the Campidoglio.*

Antiquities in the Capitol

Antiquities have been kept on the Capitoline Hill since the museums were established in 1471. Palazzo Nuovo was designed by Michelangelo and housed statues after its completion in 1654. In 1734, it became the world's first public museum.

Roman Monumentality

It was not simply the beauty and harmony of Roman architecture that inspired Renaissance architects. They admired the grandeur and scale of the Roman buildings, which seemed to echo the power and extent of the Empire itself. With the Catholic Church now matching the Roman Empire in size and scale, architects strove to introduce a fitting note of monumentality in their own works. Even private patrons benefited from this taste for magnificence.

The Campidoglio

In the late 1530s, Pope Paul III commissioned Michelangelo to restructure the buildings surrounding the Campidoglio (Capitol) on the Capitoline Hill, the civic and political heart of the city of Rome. Michelangelo added a new building and changed the façades of two existing buildings. He also added an oval design to the pavement.

▶ *This aerial view of the Capitoline Hill shows the overall effect of Michelangelo's designs.*

A Crowning Achievement

c. 1546 To quell disputes, the Pope decrees that Michelangelo should have the final say in St. Peter's construction.
1550 Michelangelo finishes the Pauline Chapel frescoes. After the death of Pope Paul III in late 1549, Julius III's short papacy begins. Publication of Giorgio Vasari's *Lives of the Most Eminent Painters, Sculptors, and Architects*, featuring much on Michelangelo.
1553 Publication of Ascanio Condivi's *Life of Michelangelo*.
1555 After Pope Julius III's death, Marcellus II is elected.

In 1546, Michelangelo agreed to become chief architect of the Basilica of St. Peter's. As he wrote to his nephew Lionardo Buonarotti: "Many believe, — and I believe — that I have been designated for this work by God. In spite of my old age, I do not want to give it up; I work out of love for God and I put all my hope in Him." Michelangelo encountered opposition to his designs, with some rivals accusing him of senility, but he was championed by the art historian Giorgio Vasari (1511–74) as well as Pope Paul III.

▼ Brunelleschi's dome for the cathedral of Florence (1420–36) was a familiar landmark as well as an inspiration for Michelangelo.

The Dome

Pope Julius II's plans for the new St. Peter's called for a massive dome, which posed many construction difficulties. The papal architect looked to Florence's Cathedral, with its huge dome, for inspiration. There the architect and engineer Filippo Brunelleschi had constructed a dome that was the largest and highest of its time. Moreover, Brunelleschi's dome had been built without a supporting frame to support the vault during construction.

▼ Pope Julius II Ordering Bramante, Michelangelo, and Raphael to Construct the Vatican and St. Peter's *(1827) by the French artist Émile-Jean-Horace Vernet (1789–1863).*

Artists and Architects

Pope Julius II was an energetic and persuasive patron of the arts. Once the pope decided to rebuild St. Peter's, he gathered all of Rome's leading artists and architects. Over the years, new plans superseded existing designs because of this meeting. The basilica would eventually be completed in 1615, long after Julius II and the leading artists, who included Michelangelo, Bramante, Raphael, Baldassare Peruzzi (1481–1536), and Antonio da Sangallo the Younger.

▲ A late medieval view of the old St. Peter's Basilica. By the fifteenth century, its walls were leaning badly, and its frescoes were covered in dust.

A History Of St. Peter's

St. Peter's Basilica commemorates the disciple who founded the Christian faith and who is considered by Catholics to have been the first pope. Its history dates back to 319 A.D., when Constantine (c. 280–337), the first Christian Roman emperor, had a basilica built on the site of St. Peter's tomb. This church stood for more than one thousand years, being constantly restored and altered until it was near collapse in the mid-fifteenth century. The reconstruction begun in 1452 was soon abandoned because of lack of money, but in 1506, Pope Julius II commissioned the architect Donato Bramante to raze the existing building and build a new basilica.

► Elevation of St.Peter's, After Michelangelo's Plan *(c. 1569) by Étienne Dupérac. Michelangelo's plans called for a broader, less steep dome than the one that finally crowned St. Peter's Basilica.*

Michelangelo's Design

Political turmoil, including the Sack of Rome in 1527, delayed plans for building St. Peter's. In 1546, Pope Paul III turned to Michelangelo, who was then more than seventy years old, to take over the design. Michelangelo wanted to return to Bramante's original idea of a church in the shape of a Greek cross with "arms" of the same length. He met resistance from architects whom he accused of being linked to Antonio da Sangallo the Younger, his predecessor. In 1549, the pope decreed that Michelangelo should have the final say, and construction continued under Michelangelo's overall command.

Bramante's Basilica

Donato Bramante was the outstanding architect of the late fifteenth and early sixteenth centuries. He developed an architectural style that was steeped in classical knowledge while working in Milan in the 1480s and 1490s. In 1503, Pope Julius II summoned Bramante to Rome to work on two enormous projects. The first was the huge courtyard of the Belvedere, but this work was overshadowed by Bramante's commission to design the new St. Peter's Basilica.

► *Bramante's plan for St. Peter's was a brilliant combination of classical harmony achieved on a grand scale. His proposed dome resembled that of Michelangelo (above) but had fewer embellishments.*

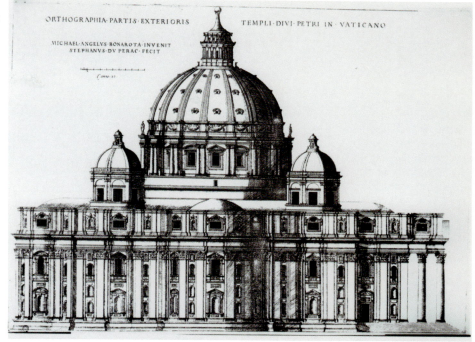

ORTHOGRAPHIA·PARTIS·EXTERIORIS   TEMPLI·DIVI·PETRI·IN·VATICANO

MICHAEL·ANGELVS·BONAROTA·INVENIT
STEPHANVS·DV·PERAC·FECIT

St. Peter's Completed

The work on St. Peter's after Michelangelo's death introduced several changes, notably the more pointed dome and the basilica's alteration to Latin-cross shape (with one longer "arm"). The basilica was consecrated in 1626 when the rebuilding was finally finished. The seventeenth-century façade was criticized because it hid the dome from viewers below.

▼ *Seen from St. Peter's Square, the basilica is an imposing structure, with Michelangelo's dome still its outstanding feature.*

▼ *This plan shows features of the completed St. Peter's Basilica within the overall Vatican complex.*

The Pigna Courtyard

The Belvedere Courtyard

St. Peter Square, laid out by Gianlorenzo Bernini (1598–1680) in the seventeenth century.

The Borgia Tower

The Sistine Chapel

Dome designed by Michelangelo

St. Peter's Basilica

The Obelisk

1556 Michelangelo begins a pilgrimage to Loreto, in the Marches region of Italy, but is called back to Rome.
1559 Pope Pius IV is elected.
1559–60 Michelangelo does designs for the church San Giovanni dei Fiorentini in Rome.
1560 Michelangelo receives commission for the Sforza Chapel in Santa Maria Maggiore, Rome.
1561 Michelangelo receives commission for the Porta Pia and Santa Maria degli Angeli, Rome.
1564 Michelangelo dies on February 18.

Sorrowful Old Age

Michelangelo lived to be eighty-nine, a long time nowadays but remarkable in the sixteenth century when life spans were much shorter. Even more remarkable was the fact that Michelangelo worked until his death, drawing and chiseling blocks of marble for his statues and overseeing architectural projects. Failing eyesight was his only real limitation. Despite his continued activity, Michelangelo found his thoughts turning more and more to death. This sorrowful turn of mind found expression in a series of religious works — both drawings and sculptures — that deal with the Passion and death of Christ.

◄ *Porta Pia, Michelangelo's last architectural project, is a testament to the artist's tenacity and enduring energy.*

Porta Pia

Remarkably, Michelangelo was still in demand as an architect when he was in his eighties. His last architectural project, commissioned by Pope Pius IV (1499–1565) in 1561, was for the renovation of the Porta Pia and the surrounding area in Rome. Michelangelo provided detailed plans for this grand gateway and the urban renewal and was able to oversee its completion just before his death in 1564.

The Grand Duke of Florence

Following Alessandro de' Medici's assassination in 1537, Florence had been ruled by Cosimo de' Medici (1519–74). Cosimo was often cruel but also proved to be enlightened, encouraging the arts and education. He shrewdly supported Spain in wider Italian politics, earning the admiration of the Vatican. In 1569, Pope Pius V made him Cosimo I, the first Grand Duke of Tuscany.

◄ *This detail from a Giorgio Vasari ceiling painting shows Cosimo being crowned as the first Grand Duke of Tuscany.*

▲ *Michelangelo's* Study for the Porta Pia *(c. 1561) shows the meticulous care and professionalism of an architect in his early twenties.*

▲ *This detail of a nineteenth-century painting by Giuseppe Ciaranfi depicts Benedetto Varchi reading his* Storia Fiorentina, *which was written for his patron, Cosimo I.*

The Crucifixion

From about 1550, at age seventy-five, Michelangelo devoted himself increasingly to pious and sorrowful religious studies. Although still physically strong — Vasari described how he could still cleave a block of marble with a single blow — Michelangelo suffered from failing eyesight. The result, evident in his last drawings, serves to add to their sense of melancholy and sadness. Many of Michelangelo's works from this time deal with the Passion and death of Christ, a subject that captivated him.

▲ *A chalk study of* Christ on the Cross between the Virgin and St. John the Evangelist *(c. 1556).*

Benedetto Varchi

Benedetto Varchi (1503-65) was a Florentine poet and historian who charted much of Florence's turbulent sixteenth-century history. Varchi had fought against the Medici in 1530 and again in 1536, but he was pardoned by Cosimo and commissioned to write a history of the city — the sixteen-volume *Storia Fiorentina* (History of Florence). Varchi sent Michelangelo transcripts of his lectures at the Accademia Fiorentina (including one about Michelangelo's sonnets). The two men exchanged letters comparing the arts of painting and sculpture. Varchi delivered the eulogy at Michelangelo's funeral.

▶ *The sad, serene face of Nicodemus in the* Florentine Pietà *is considered by some to be Michelangelo's self-portrait.*

A Personal Pietà

Michelangelo's first biographers, Vasari and Condivi, wrote that the sculptor began the *Florentine Pietà* to adorn his own tomb, which he wanted to be in the church of Santa Maria Maggiore in Rome. For unknown reasons, Michelangelo destroyed parts of the sculpture in 1555. It was retouched by Michelangelo's assistant, Tiberio Calcagni (1532–65), especially the figure of Mary Magdalene on Christ's right. There is a sense of profound sadness in the positioning of Nicodemus, the Virgin, and Mary Magdalene as they struggle with Christ's lifeless body. Despite that, the sculpture displays an astounding sense of real movement and physical tension.

1564 Michelangelo dies in Rome but is buried in Florence.
1568 Vasari's second edition of *Lives of the Most Eminent Painters, Sculptors, and Architects* is published.
1979 Initial tests are conducted to begin restoration of the Sistine Chapel frescoes.
1980 Work begins on the Sistine Chapel restoration.
1996 A controversy develops over the attribution of the Manhattan *Cupid*.
1999 Pope John Paul II celebrates Mass in the Sistine Chapel to mark the end of the fresco restoration program.
2002 The controversial cleaning of the *David* begins.

The Legacy of Michelangelo

At the time of his death, Michelangelo's reputation was already secure, both in the great works he had completed and in the influence he had had on contemporary artists such as Raphael and Titian and the Venetian School. Like his fellow Florentine and sometime rival Leonardo da Vinci, Michelangelo earned the term "Renaissance Man" because of the breadth of his talents and interests. His artistic triumphs are viewed afresh by each generation. Beyond the list of his masterpieces is something else that Michelangelo passed on as a legacy. Born into a world where artists were still considered virtually workmen, he left it as an example of individual artistic genius.

Michelangelo's Sonnets

Michelangelo was a difficult person to understand or perhaps even to like, but like other Renaissance artists, he enjoyed reading and writing poetry. His preferred form of poetry was the sonnet, a carefully constructed fourteen-line poem following a set rhyme scheme. Within the self-imposed strict confines of the sonnet, he expressed his view of himself far more openly than he ever could with his painting or sculpture. Many of Michelangelo's poems deal with art and the difficulties he faced in producing his great works, poking fun at patrons and critics alike. Others, however, showed him to be a keen student of philosophy and someone devoted to intense friendships and spiritual relationships.

Michelangelo's Tomb

Thanks to the published work of Vasari and Condivi, Michelangelo had become a legend in his own lifetime. Upon his death in 1564, Michelangelo would be the subject of a major dispute. Michelangelo himself had originally intended to be buried in the church of Santa Maria Maggiore in Rome, but his brief will made no mention of this resting place. Instead, preparations were made to bury him in St. Peter's. Michelangelo's nephew Lionardo, claiming that Michelangelo had wanted to be buried in Florence, spirited the artist's remains to his native city. There he was laid to rest in the church of Santa Croce.

▶ *Michelangelo's elaborate tomb (1564–c. 1572) in Santa Croce, Florence, was created by his great admirer, Giorgio Vasari.*

Giorgio Vasari

Giorgio Vasari was an accomplished painter and architect, but he is best remembered for his work as a biographer. Like his contemporary Ascanio Condivi (who published the Life of Michelangelo in 1553), Vasari supplied biographical information in the wider context of art history. In his great work, *Lives of the Most Eminent Painters, Sculptors, and Architects* (1550), Vasari argued that Tuscan artists, beginning with Giotto and Cimabue (c. 1240–1302), revived the traditions of true art and that the Renaissance marked the real flowering of this artistic revival.

▼ *Self-Portrait (1567) by Vasari. He chose Michelangelo as the only living artist to be included in his great work.*

◄ *This statue, believed to be the work of Michelangelo, was rediscovered in 1996 in the cultural offices of the French embassy in New York.*

The Swiss Guards

Michelangelo is popularly believed to have designed the distinctive uniform of the Swiss Guards, but there is no proof of his involvement. The Swiss Guards, who act as papal bodyguards, were founded in 1505. Invaders occupied and damaged the Vatican during the Sack of Rome in 1527, but the Swiss Guards helped Pope Clement VII to safety in Castel Sant'Angelo. The company normally comprises 107 men, all of whom must be Swiss, Roman Catholic, unmarried, and handsome.

▶ *The Swiss Guards guard the gates into Vatican City and escort the pope on special occasions in St. Peter's.*

The Restoration of the Sistine Chapel Frescoes

The 1980s and early 1990s saw one of the most publicized — and controversial — art restoration projects in history. Beginning in 1980, restorers worked to remove nearly five hundred years' worth of soot that had accumulated on Michelangelo's Sistine Chapel frescoes. The soot was produced by votive candles that have burned day and night since the frescoes were completed. The project took nineteen years, beginning with the ceiling and finishing with *The Last Judgment* in 1999. The work revealed the brightness of the original coloring, which had been darkened over time. Some critics protested, claiming that Michelangelo had actually covered the frescoes with a varnish to darken them.

▼ *A computer mounted 65 feet (20 m) above the ground assisted restorers in their efforts to remove the accumulated soot from Michelangelo's frescoes.*

The Case of the Manhattan Cupid

In 1996, art historian Kathleen Weil-Garris Brandt became convinced that a statue of Cupid in the French embassy in New York had been carved by Michelangelo. Although the same claim had been made by an Italian writer in 1968, no one had paid attention. Brandt concluded that Michelangelo had carved the statue to replace the fake classical sculpture he had made when he first arrived in Rome in 1496 (see page 15). The art world remains divided about the explanation, but the incident highlights how difficult it is to attribute the works of Michelangelo, who signed only one piece — the *Pietà* in St. Peter's Basilica (see page 17).

Glossary

apprentice A person who is under agreement to serve, for a specified period of time, a person skilled in a trade. In the Renaissance, boys seeking to become artists received their training by serving as apprentices in the workshops of established artists.

attribute To credit an artist with the creation of a work of art.

Baroque Of or related to the heavily ornamented style of European art of the seventeenth century.

Basilica A Catholic church where special ceremonies can take place, or one of the seven major Roman churches founded in ancient times.

bay A major section or part into which a building or architectural structure is divided.

cartoon A full-sized preparatory drawing used to transfer a design to a wall.

classical Term used to describe works of art from ancient Greece or Rome, or works which have the same characteristics as the works of ancient Greece or Rome.

commission The act of appointing someone to do a specified task, or the actual task or duty given to someone under an agreement. Artists in the Renaissance usually signed contracts that stipulated salary and other details pertinent to the work to be produced when they received commissions.

Counter-Reformation The movement of the Catholic Church against the Protestant Reformation in the sixteenth to early seventeenth centuries that sought to strengthen the Catholic Church.

courtier A noble who served and was a member of the court of a king or ruler.

excommunication The act of punishing a member of the Catholic Church by forcing him or her out of active participation.

façade The front part of a building.

fresco painting A mural painting made by the application of color onto a wall whose top layer of plaster is still wet.

guild An association representing a certain trade or craft in medieval and Renaissance Europe.

heresy An opinion or belief held against an established doctrine of the Catholic Church or an official religion.

Humanism A cultural movement of the fifteenth century based on the study of classical texts, or a system of thought concerned with the needs of man rather than with those of religion.

indulgence A pardon granted by the Catholic Church that gave one freedom from punishment or guilt of sins.

lunette A decorated semicircular space on a wall or ceiling.

Mannerism An Italian art movement or style of the sixteenth century that broke away from the ideals of classical art with the distortion of forms and the use of bright colors.

militia An army made up of ordinary citizens or nonprofessional soldiers.

monarchy A form of government or state ruled by a king or queen.

Neoplatonism A school of ancient Greek philosophy (practiced in ancient times and later in the Renaissance) that revived the ideas of the philosopher Plato.

palazzo Italian word for building or palace.

patron A person or group of people that gives money to a person or group to perform a certain task or for some other worthy purpose.

patron saint A holy man or woman who is believed to protect a particular group or community.

pendentive A concave triangular space formed by the intersection of two arches at the base of a domed or vaulted structure.

perspective The method of representing objects so as to make them appear three-dimensional. The illusion of depth and space or a view extending far into the distance.

Pietà Term used to refer to a work of art that depicts the Virgin Mary holding the dead body of Christ.

porta A gateway into a town of ancient or medieval origins, usually marked by an arched architectural opening in the walls surrounding the town.

portal A large doorway or elaborate entrance.

Protestant A member of any Christian Church or community that separated itself from the Catholic Church during the Reformation.

Reformation The European religious movement of the sixteenth century that aimed to improve the practices of the Catholic Church but ultimately led to the branching off of the Protestant Church.

Renaissance The cultural movement, originating in Italy during fourteenth century and lasting until the seventeenth century, in which the art, literature, and ideas of ancient Greece were rediscovered and applied to the arts. The artistic style of this period.

sacristy A small room in a church where priests prepare for ceremonies and where holy objects or official records are kept. A sacristy can also be a part of a church building where prayer meetings or other church functions are conducted.

scaffolding A system or set of platforms erected around a structure being repaired or painted for workmen to stand on when working high above the ground.

treatise A literary work, a book or article, in which an author expresses an opinion about a subject by examining its principles and treating them with a planned and organized discussion.

vault An arched roof or ceiling.

villa A large estate or residence located in the country or outside a town.

workshop A place where heavy work is carried out, a factory. In the Renaissance, an artist's workshop was run by a master artist who, with the help of various apprentices and assistants, produced works of art. The master artist directed the organization and production of his own workshop.

Index

Aldovrandi, Giovan Francesco 13
Alberti, Leon Battista 24
   On Painting 24
Aristotle 25

Baldassare del Milanese 15
Battle of Anghiari 17
Bernini, Gianlorenzo 41
Bertoldo di Giovanni 10
Bologna 6, 9, 12, 13, 14, 18
Borgia family 14
   Cesare 16
   Rodrigo de see Pope Alexander VI
Botticelli, Sandro 6, 8, 9, 11, 20
   Birth of Venus, The 6
   Scenes from the Life of Moses 22
Bracciolini, Poggio 38
Bramante, Donato 19, 20, 38, 41
   Plan for the dome of St. Peter's
      Basilica 41
Brunelleschi, Filippo 29, 40
Buonarroti family
   Buonarotto (younger brother of
      Michelangelo) 20
   Lionardo (nephew of
      Michelangelo) 40, 44
   Lodovico (father of
      Michelangelo) 8

Calcagni, Tiberio 43
Caprese 6
Carrara 14, 18, 19
Castiglione, Baldassare 28
   Book of the Courtier, The 28
Catholicism 26
Catholics 14, 36, 40
Charles V (Holy Roman Emperor,
   King Charles I of Spain) 30, 31, 33
Charles VIII (king of France) 12, 13
Christ 15, 20, 32, 42, 43
Christianity 35, 36
Church (Catholic) 14, 26, 36, 37,
   38, 39
Ciaranfi, Giuseppe 43
Colonna, Vittoria 6, 36, 37
Columbus, Christopher 12
Condivi, Ascanio 24, 43, 44, 45
   Life of Michelangelo 40
Constantine, Emperor of Rome
   39, 40
Copernicus, Nicolaus, 36, 37
   *On the Revolution of Heavenly
      Bodies* 37
Council of Trent 36
Counter-Reformation 36, 37

da Vinci, Leonardo 11, 17, 44
Della Robbia 16
Dominican Order 13
Donatello 10
   David 10
Doni, Agnolo 7, 17
Dupérac, Étienne 41
   *Elevation of St. Peter's, After
      Michelangelo's Plan* 41

Europe 7, 28

Farnese family 35
Ferdinand II (king of Spain) 12
Ficino, Marsilio 10
Florence 6, 7, 8, 9, 12, 14, 16, 17, 18,
20, 23, 27, 28, 29, 31, 32, 38, 43, 44
   Accademia Fiorentina 43
   Cathedral 16, 18, 40
   Galleria dell'Accademia 18
   Great Council 16
   Medici Chapels 29
   Palazzo Medici Riccardi 7, 8
   Palazzo Vecchio (Palazzo dell
      Signoria) 16, 17
   Republic 6, 16, 31
   San Lorenzo 29, 30
   San Miniato al Monte 31
   Santa Croce 9, 44
   Santa Maria Novella 7, 8, 9
   Santo Spirito 12
   Via Borgognona 7
   Via Larga 7
   Via Ghibellina 7
Florin 7
Fra' Bartolomeo 13
   Portrait of Girolamo Savonarola 13
France 16, 19, 33
French (people) 13, 16
fresco painting 25

Germany 33, 36
Ghirlandaio
   Benedetto 8
   Davide 8
   Domenico 8, 9, 20
   workshop 6, 8, 10
Giotto 9, 10
   Ascension of John the Evangelist 9
Granacci, Francesco 10
Greece (ancient) 10, 25, 37
guilds 16
Holy Roman Emperor 16
Holy Roman Empire 33
Humanism 10

Index, The 36
Isabella I (queen of Spain) 12
Italy see also individual regions and
   cities 6, 13, 18, 22, 28, 33, 42

Jesuit Order see Society of Jesus
Julius Caesar 38

Lagraulas, Cardinal Bilheres de 14
Laocoön group 18
Loreto, Italy 42
Loyola, Ignatius 36
Luther, Martin 24, 36

Machiavelli, Niccolò 16, 28
   The Prince 16
Mannerism 32
Marches (region of Italy) 42
Mary Magdalene 41
Masaccio 9
   Brancacci Chapel frescoes 9
Medici Family 6, 8, 10, 13, 16, 27, 28,
   29, 30, 31, 38, 43
   Alessandro 31, 42
   Cardinal see Pope Clement VII
   Cosimo (the Elder) 10, 29
   Cosimo I (Grand Duke of Tuscany)
      42, 43
   Giovanni see Pope Leo X
   Giuliano 28
   Giulio see Pope Clement VII
   Lorenzo (the Magnificent) 6, 10,
      11, 12, 27, 28, 29, 30
   Lorenzo 28
   Piero 12, 13, 16, 28
   Villa at Cafaggiolo 8
Melozzo da Forlì 20
   Portrait of Sixtus IV 20
Michelangelo
   Angel Bearing a Candlestick 13
   Apostles 16, 18
   *Ascension of John the Evangelist
      after Giotto* 9
   Bacchus 14, 15
   Battle of the Centaurs, The 11
   Bruges Madonna 18
   Battle of Cascina 17
   Battle of the Centaurs, The 11
   Brutus 38
   Campidoglio 39
   *Christ on the Cross between the
      Virgin and St. John the
      Evangelist* 43
   Crucifix 12
   David 6, 16, 17, 18, 44
   Florentine Pietà (1550) 41

Index

Holy Family with St. John the Baptist (Doni Tondo) 7, 17
Last Judgment, The 6, 7, 32, 34, 35, 45
Laurentian (Medici) Library 30, 31
Madonna of the Stairs 10
Manhattan *Cupid* 44, 45
Medici Madonna 6
New Sacristy 28, 29, 30
    Dawn and *Dusk* 29
    Medici Tombs 30
nude figure 12
Palazzo Farnese 39
Pauline Chapel frescoes 37, 38
    The Conversion of St. Paul 37
Pietà (1501) 6, 9, 15, 15, 18
Plans for the Fortifications of the Porta al Prato di Ognissanti 31
Risen Christ 26
San Lorenzo façade 6, 28, 29
Sistine Chapel ceiling frescoes 7, 21, 22–23, 45
    Creation of Adam, The 21
    Sybil of Delphi, The 21
Sleeping Cupid 15
Sonnets 44
St. Matthew 18
St. Peter's Basilica dome 41
Study for the Porta Pia 42
Tomb of Pope Julius II 6, 19, 26, 27, 28, 30, 38
    Bound Slave 26
Tondo Pitti 17
Michelozzo 8
Milan 41
Milanese (people) 17
Moors 12
Moses 20

Naples, Kingdom of 13
Neoplatonism 10
Nero, Emperor of Rome 18
Netherlands 33
New World 12
Nicodemus 43

Old Testament 7, 24

Papal States 14, 19
Paris, France
    Louvre Museum 26
Perugia 25
Perugino, Pietro 8, 20, 35
Peruzzi, Baldassare 40
Pisa 13
    Cascina 17

Pisans (people) 17
Pitti, Bartolommeo 17
Plato 10, 25
Platonic Academy 10
Pontormo, Jacobo 33
    Deposition 33
popes
    Alexander VI 13, 14, 16, 18, 19
    Clement VII 28, 30, 31, 35, 45
    John Paul II 45
    Julius II 6, 7, 16, 18, 19, 20, 24, 25, 40, 41
    Julius III 40
    Leo X 27, 28
    Marcellus II 40
    Paul III 32, 35, 36, 39, 40, 41
    Pius III 19
    Pius IV 42
    Sixtus IV 20
Protestants 26, 30, 33, 36

Raphael 19, 24, 25, 44
    Portrait of Castiglione 28
    Portrait of Pope Julius II 19
    Portrait of Pope Leo X 27
    School of Athens 25
    Self-Portrait 25
Reformation 14, 26, 32, 35, 36, 37
Riario, Cardinal Raffaele 14, 15
Ridolfi, Cardinal Niccolò 38
Roman Empire 14, 33, 39
Romans (people) 18
Rome 6, 7, 9, 14, 18, 22, 24, 30, 31, 32, 36, 38, 39, 40, 42, 44
    ancient 10, 37
    Campidoglio (Capitol) 38, 39
    Capitoline Hill 38, 39
    Castel Sant'Angelo 33, 45
    Colosseum 14
    Il Gesù 36
    Macel' de' Corvi 26
    Palazzo Farnese 38, 39
    Pantheon 38
    Porta Pia 42
    Sack of 33, 41, 45
    San Giovanni dei Fiorentini 42
    San Pietro in Vincoli 27
    Santa Maria Maggiore 42, 43, 44
        Sforza Chapel 42
    Santa Maria Sopra Minerva 26
Rosselli, Francesco di Lorenzo 7

Sangallo family 38
    Antonio the Younger 39, 40, 41
    Bastiano 17

Savonarola, Girolamo 12, 13, 14, 16, 28
Settignano 7, 8
Siena 16
    Piccolomini altar 16
Signorelli, Luca 8, 20
Society of Jesus (Jesuit Order) 36
Soderini, Piero 28
Spain 12, 14, 28, 33, 42
Swiss Guards 45

Taddei, Taddeo 17
Tornabuoni, Giovanni 9
Tuscany 19, 42
    Grand Duchy of 31

Vannini, Ottavio 11
Varchi, Benedetto 43
    Storia Fiorentina 43
Vasari, Giorgio 31, 40, 42, 43, 44, 45
    Leo X Entering Florence 28
    Lives of the Most Eminent Italian Architects, Painters, and Sculptors 40, 44, 45
    Self-Portrait 45
Vatican 14, 18, 20, 24, 25, 28, 41, 42
    Papal Palace 32
    Sistine Chapel 6, 18, 20, 21, 24, 25, 26, 32, 36, 41, 44
    St. Peter's Basilica 6, 14, 15, 18, 19, 26, 27, 40, 41, 44, 45
Venice 12
Vernet, Émile-Jean-Horace 40
    Pope Julius II Ordering Bramante, Michelangelo, and Raphael to Construct the Vatican and St. Peter's 40
Verrocchio, Andrea del 11
Vespucci, Amerigo 12
Virgin (Mary) 9, 15, 17, 32, 43
Vitruvius, Marcus 38
    On Architecture 38
Volterra, Daniele da 6